Spare, both episodic and epigrammatic, a
quotidian, Brittany Tomaselli's *Since Sun*
book of hours—except for hours, insert anxieties. What to do about
seeing in one's face "a strange absence of plot," or when the speaker,
having once owned a crystal ball, finds that "it's gone and I'm afraid to
look for it because I don't want it to be really lost?" One answer, the
poems suggest, is to record everything—from which neighborhood
dogs are out or aren't, to the lone pine in the middle of the city; to make
record of the exterior side by side with an interior beset with anxiety, to
give plot to what feels plotless, to establish points of navigation and in
doing so to make of anxiety, if only for now, a crossable space like any
other. "I wish I were/composed of wind and/2 fine birds each/holding a
perfectly folded square map," writes Tomaselli—maps tell us both where
we are and how to find where we aren't. Wind is what carries the birds,
who no longer need the maps they carry (hence the maps being folded).
These poems seem the wind's equivalent, offering a way through fear, past
doubt, to the stay of belief, in the self, and in each small life's possibilities.
Tomaselli is a marvel. I'm so grateful for *Since Sunday*.

Carl Phillips, author of *Wild is the Wind*
and judge of the Omnidawn Poetry Chapbook Prize

Since Sunday is one of the most remarkable collections I've read in a
long time—it's a chapbook as big as the sky. This is actual seeing—
what poetry forgot—and antennae-accurate hearing, which it can't
live without. With singular candor and deftness, Brittany Tomaselli
summons a world on every page, like a mage with her scrying
sphere—so she is. Hatless men, Reader, all—delight. Everything in
Since Sunday is alive.

Lisa Fishman, author of *24 Pages and other poems*

Since Sunday

Since Sunday

Brittany Tomaselli

Omnidawn Publishing
Oakland, California
2019

Cover Art: *Untitled* by Michael Zhang
www.michaelzhangdesign.com. @mzhangart

Cover and Interior set in Palatino LT Std and Garamond Premier Pro

Cover and Interior design by Trisha Peck

Printed in the United States
by Books International, Dulles, Virginia
On 55# Glatfelter B19 Antique
Acid Free Archival Quality Recycled Paper

Library of Congress Cataloging-in-Publication Data

Names: Tomaselli, Brittany, 1991- author.
Title: Since Sunday / Brittany Tomaselli.
Description: Oakland, California : Omnidawn Publishing, 2019.
Identifiers: LCCN 2019017404 | ISBN 9781632430731 (paperback : acid-free paper)
Subjects: | BISAC: POETRY / General. | POETRY / American / General.
Classification: LCC PS3620.O4756 A6 2019 | DDC 811/.6--dc23
LC record available at https://lccn.loc.gov/2019017404

Published by Omnidawn Publishing, Oakland, California
www.omnidawn.com (510) 237-5472 (800) 792-4957
10 9 8 7 6 5 4 3 2 1
ISBN: 978-1-63243-073-1

CONTENTS

On the twelfth, I am taking the train. A man in a large dark suit has a colorful checkered tie and the colors move diagonally across it. His sunglasses are round and small. To my left there are two pairs of blue and tan seats with silver metal bars. One pair in front of the other, they face the opposite way of me. A man sits in the right seat of each pair. Both men are closing their eyes.

Hatless men,   I want to tell you   this train is not the autumn wind

Now what should I remember. That was Thursday, but I'm much better now. The green construction vehicle is pulling a tractor and I know that no one is back at home. I'm eating a chocolate scone and thinking what I can command. I would like to walk a dog or ride a bike. Please come meet me.

Understandable: lights blinking quickly each second it's dusk

The kind that are now a wilderness or even a small house

It's easier to catch two
giant frogs than hatch one
egg in your sock drawer

Just stay confident
bees get caught in your hair
all the time

I used to be small
and very loved.   At the hot air balloon festival

I was afraid.

My knees turn violet when cold.

My young skin was

sometimes   in the rain.

Every morning while washing my face there's a strange absence of plot.

Then I am driving around a very old woman. She keeps asking me to turn into the cemetery to go see her dead husband but I keep forgetting to turn in time. She doesn't mind because I have on a very boring radio show where a man keeps talking and even though it isn't biblical, he makes it sound biblical. It is beautiful outside.

Some burden is lifted
while chewing on bread.
I need to be more and less patient with myself.

Once I found a quarter by the lake.
Anxiety as anxiety or garden—
which is an abbreviation for people.

I can't bring myself to use the enormous latch. You came into the fall
playing solitaire.

Darling needles and black wool curtain hats in my head

The only reason I am so careful:

Well yes god,
I have an old bed

I often wake up feeling like 2 or 3 people are watching me
woven in among the straw flowers
An uncommon mixture
in an enormous park

There are an awful lot of papers on this desk.

The answer to the riddle was *birds*.

I won't eat the crumbs on the aluminum foil
because I know the sound that foil makes.

Today I'm going to work the way I did
yesterday.   A red trolley

had rounded black windows there were lights.

I wish I were
composed of wind and
                2 fine birds each
                        holding a perfectly folded square map.

It's mostly a glass surface; it is blue and reflects the lights. The bottom is a curved line that attaches to the two sides. The two sides go straight up and remain parallel until about three inches up where it starts to curve in toward each other. At its thinnest, the object is about an inch in diameter while at its largest, it is about two. Above the thinnest part there is a slightly larger rim which attaches to a black plastic surface. The lines on the side of the black surface are parallel to each other and are about 1 ½ inches across. Above that is a black rubber dome. The dome shape is about 1 ¾ inches tall. The very top part reflects the light as well.

Stop doing evil
things pope tells mafia
under a bridge in Venice.
Which is sinking.

I've heard the gondola drivers must still
exemplify something forgotten, something
you'd pay to watch sink. If sea level is
zero, then what.

Saw the women with the spotted dog in the alley
but the three greyhounds in their colorful cloaks aren't out yet

Since Sunday, I've gained another cut on the part of my finger I type with. Should I become a faux internet psychic? I need to make money and I'd like a new name. I owned a crystal ball (actually a small black obsidian scrying sphere) but it's gone and I'm afraid to look for it because I don't want it to be really lost.

The day's a ghost that sits down:

it's better we not think about him.
What's all this fuss about flowers?

Who's afraid here,

me or you?

We could walk for hours from the table to the bed and never find
the way out.

She went inside the house:

This is furniture, she said,

nobody lives here.

The ability to smile
is not the same thing as

If doubt became bewildered,

would there suddenly be relief?

       Later: some were seen rowing boats through a rain
                 that coiled around the earth.

Ashamed, altogether she became a plum in an-
other pagoda.

The sky, it seems, is often blocking the birds.

My own   in twos, build supper-lands.
My lost four lives turned crisp south hue.

Whether he has a gun or the door does not open
your arms out on a stone pillar while talking

The garden went or jumped slow
don't forget

Her off-hand cried
a much larger dark brown bird

Where should I have hidden

Now that the ocean is gone,
there is nothing better

than being a child
in a cornfield,
she believes.

Ever thought of being in the movies? Well, in Texas your beauty is worth diamonds. You won't even need to kiss anyone. Susie Q, you need to get yourself a marine. But guess what. All the marines are at the Navy Pier. Down at the Build-a Bear! And honey, you're in the psych ward. Do you wear a string bikini? Do you like dolphins? Otters? Groundhogs? Well in South Padre you can rescue them or not, and then head to the tiki bar. I fight like a rich person: I cause riots, which keep everyone from being raped. They're not getting dialysis when they need it, and you know, cell phones are the number one cause of rape. But there aren't any rapes in Maui. Listen Susie Q! I'm pregnant. And bit by a brown recluse spider. I spent fifty two days having my first daughter. I was ready to do it again. So I took a huge mallet and knocked down all the walls in my house. And then we didn't have heat.

What have I got to do with the night

fish spines

tiny little orchids

three thousand empty arches

Whether I said yes or

What will be different about you tomorrow
There is a white curtain in each and every window

In the middle of the city, I find the lone tree called Lookout Pine. It is a marker of an old something or other from a long time ago. From here I see all the buildings. One is a tan color and most of the windows are dark. It seems there are too many stories to count, but the fourth or fifth floor down there is a crimson colored thing (an umbrella or possibly a flag). It's only because of the contrast I can actually see the white railing in front of it.

A loud whistle against this darkening sky,   I stay beneath my pine

Dear once or twice hit,

A red pickup truck on State Street drove by filled with buckets of
marigolds. How admirable. Everyone is clapping. I'm awfully busy
with measurements. Here. Have one for distance traveled by wind or
waves. I just want to do something well.

I like this view though because.

I wish it would be cherry season   against all decree
the hilly figures are moving backwards again.

Don't move that table.

And not the old thing sitting on the couch.

Now   trotting this way like that for those,

they painted giant eyes on the engine.

How to make something:

If how said always seems unwise, whittle it forever.
Impervious letters take time yelling about lopsided.

Do tell me which I've sown eventually.

Kettle, obsidian, fluorite, amethyst, tiger's eye, alabaster, opal.
Tinúviel. Another silent animal from the past tipping the woodstove.
Can't only open things. All grief slays best.

Leery preaching lamps wobble my bedside. My window doesn't
notice the big "S." Won't nozzles stay true? Want nothing
presupposed to fly.

Tiger lily, roses, myrrh, opium, lavender, frankincense, coriander,
cloves.

ACKNOWLEDGMENTS

"Ever thought of being in the movies?" was published in *Columbia Poetry Review*.

"Now that the ocean is gone" was published in *Columbia Poetry Review*.

"Some burden is lifted" was published in *The Wanderer*.

"Dear once or twice hit" was published in *The Wanderer*.

"I like this view though because" was published in *The Wanderer*.

"Whether he has a gun or the door does not open" was published in *The Wanderer*.

"What have I got to do with the night?" was published in *The Wanderer*.

"Ashamed, altogether" was published in *The Wanderer*.

"Today I'm going to work the way I did" was published in *The Wanderer*.

"How to make something" was published in *The Wanderer*.

Brittany Tomaselli received her MFA in Poetry from Columbia College Chicago. Her work can be found in *Fairy Tale Review*, *The Wanderer*, and *Columbia Poetry Review*. She currently lives and works in Kalamazoo, Michigan.